Detailed Planning for Detail Oriented People

A Weekly Planner

Activinotes

DAILY JOURNALS, PLANNERS, NOTEBOOKS AND OTHER BLANK BOOKS

Weekly Planner

Weekly Planner

Monday

To Do :

Notes :

Tuesday

To Do :

Notes :

Wednesday

To Do :

Notes :

Thursday

To Do :

Notes :

Weekly Planner

Friday

To Do :

Notes :

_____
_____
_____
_____
_____
_____
_____
_____
_____
_____

Saturday

To Do :

Notes :

_____
_____
_____
_____
_____
_____
_____
_____
_____
_____

Sunday

To Do :

Notes :

_____
_____
_____
_____
_____
_____
_____
_____

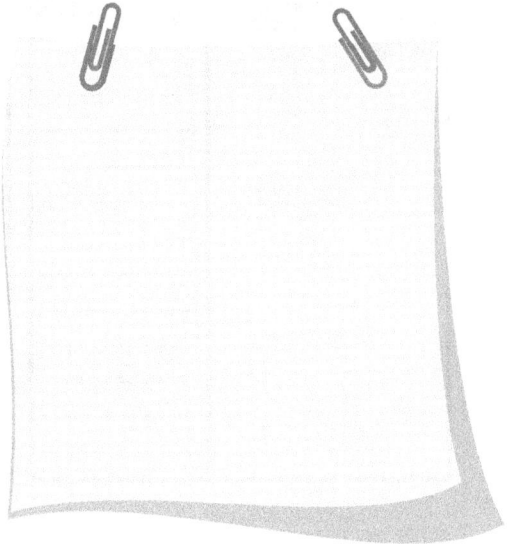

_____
_____
_____
_____
_____
_____

Weekly Planner

Monday

To Do :

Notes :

Tuesday

To Do :

Notes :

Wednesday

To Do :

Notes :

Thursday

To Do :

Notes :

Weekly Planner

Friday

To Do :

Notes :
_____
_____
_____
_____
_____
_____
_____
_____
_____
_____

Saturday

To Do :

Notes :
_____
_____
_____
_____
_____
_____
_____
_____
_____
_____

Sunday

To Do :

Notes :
_____
_____
_____
_____
_____
_____
_____
_____

_____
_____
_____
_____
_____
_____

Weekly Planner

Monday

To Do :

Notes :

Tuesday

To Do :

Notes :

Wednesday

To Do :

Notes :

Thursday

To Do :

Notes :

Weekly Planner

Friday

To Do:

Notes:

_____
_____
_____
_____
_____
_____
_____
_____
_____

Saturday

To Do:

Notes:

_____
_____
_____
_____
_____
_____
_____
_____
_____

Sunday

To Do:

Notes:

_____
_____
_____
_____
_____
_____
_____
_____

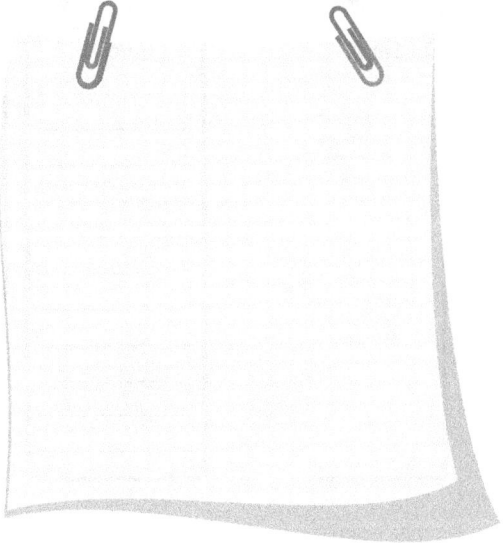

_____
_____
_____
_____
_____
_____

Weekly Planner

Monday

To Do :	Notes :

Tuesday

To Do :	Notes :

Wednesday

To Do :	Notes :

Thursday

To Do :	Notes :

Weekly Planner

Friday

To Do :	Notes :
	_____
	_____
	_____
	_____
	_____
	_____
	_____
	_____
	_____
	_____

Saturday

To Do :	Notes :
	_____
	_____
	_____
	_____
	_____
	_____
	_____
	_____
	_____
	_____

Sunday

To Do :	Notes :
	_____
	_____
	_____
	_____
	_____
	_____
	_____
	_____

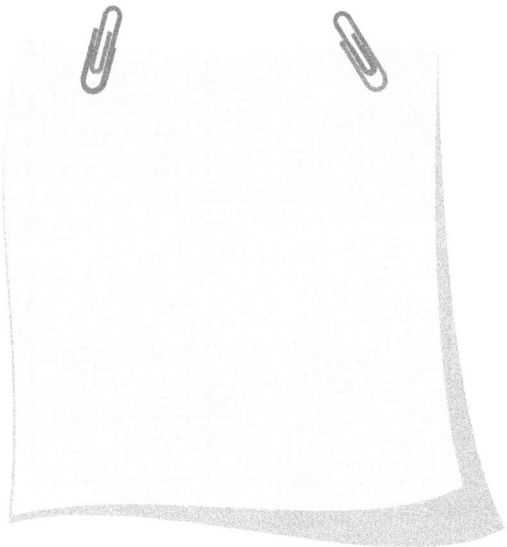

_____

_____

_____

_____

_____

_____

Weekly Planner

Monday

To Do :

Notes :

Tuesday

To Do :

Notes :

Wednesday

To Do :

Notes :

Thursday

To Do :

Notes :

Weekly Planner

Friday

To Do :

Notes :

_____
_____
_____
_____
_____
_____
_____
_____
_____
_____

Saturday

To Do :

Notes :

_____
_____
_____
_____
_____
_____
_____
_____
_____
_____

Sunday

To Do :

Notes :

_____
_____
_____
_____
_____
_____
_____
_____

_____
_____
_____
_____
_____
_____

Weekly Planner

Monday

To Do :

Notes :

Tuesday

To Do :

Notes :

Wednesday

To Do :

Notes :

Thursday

To Do :

Notes :

Weekly Planner

Friday

To Do :

Notes :

_____
_____
_____
_____
_____
_____
_____
_____
_____

Saturday

To Do :

Notes :

_____
_____
_____
_____
_____
_____
_____
_____
_____

Sunday

To Do :

Notes :

_____
_____
_____
_____
_____
_____
_____
_____

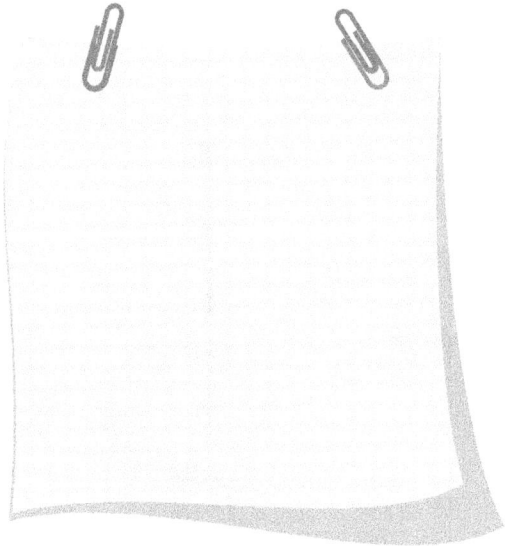

_____
_____
_____
_____
_____
_____

Weekly Planner

Monday

To Do :

Notes :

Tuesday

To Do :

Notes :

Wednesday

To Do :

Notes :

Thursday

To Do :

Notes :

Weekly Planner

Friday

To Do :

Notes :
_____
_____
_____
_____
_____
_____
_____
_____
_____
_____
_____

Saturday

To Do :

Notes :
_____
_____
_____
_____
_____
_____
_____
_____
_____
_____
_____

Sunday

To Do :

Notes :
_____
_____
_____
_____
_____
_____
_____
_____
_____
_____
_____

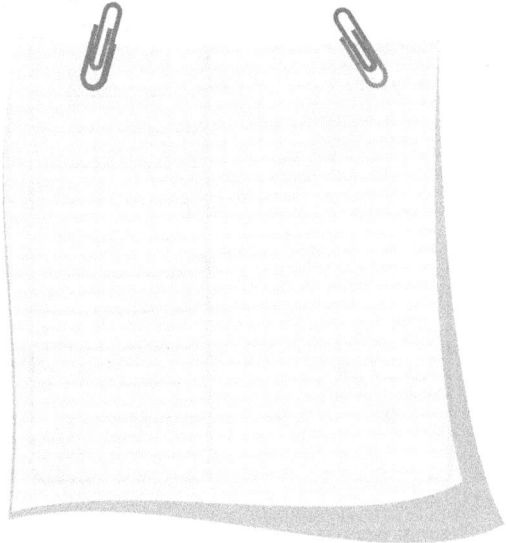

_____
_____
_____
_____
_____
_____

Weekly Planner

Monday
To Do :

Notes :

Tuesday
To Do :

Notes :

Wednesday
To Do :

Notes :

Thursday
To Do :

Notes :

Weekly Planner

Friday

To Do :

Notes :
_____
_____
_____
_____
_____
_____
_____
_____
_____
_____

Saturday

To Do :

Notes :
_____
_____
_____
_____
_____
_____
_____
_____
_____
_____

Sunday

To Do :

Notes :
_____
_____
_____
_____
_____
_____
_____
_____
_____

_____
_____
_____
_____
_____
_____

Weekly Planner

Monday

To Do :

Notes :

Tuesday

To Do :

Notes :

Wednesday

To Do :

Notes :

Thursday

To Do :

Notes :

Weekly Planner

Friday

To Do:

Notes:
_____
_____
_____
_____
_____
_____
_____
_____
_____
_____
_____
_____

Saturday

To Do:

Notes:
_____
_____
_____
_____
_____
_____
_____
_____
_____
_____
_____
_____

Sunday

To Do:

Notes:
_____
_____
_____
_____
_____
_____
_____
_____
_____

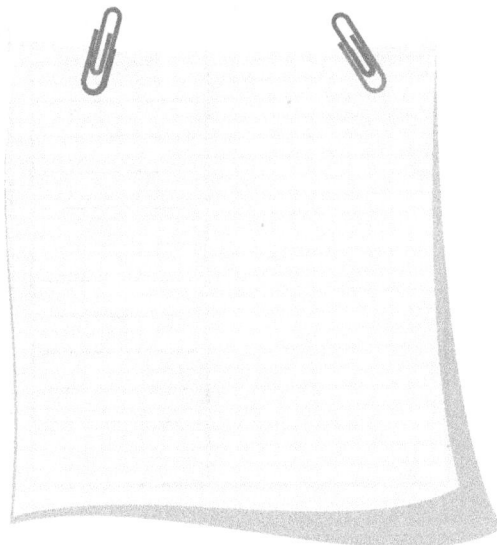

_____
_____
_____
_____
_____
_____

Weekly Planner

Monday

To Do :

Notes :

Tuesday

To Do :

Notes :

Wednesday

To Do :

Notes :

Thursday

To Do :

Notes :

Weekly Planner

Friday

To Do :

Notes :

_____
_____
_____
_____
_____
_____
_____
_____
_____
_____

Saturday

To Do :

Notes :

_____
_____
_____
_____
_____
_____
_____
_____
_____
_____

Sunday

To Do :

Notes :

_____
_____
_____
_____
_____
_____
_____
_____
_____
_____

_____
_____
_____
_____
_____
_____

Weekly Planner

Monday

To Do :

Notes :

Tuesday

To Do :

Notes :

Wednesday

To Do :

Notes :

Thursday

To Do :

Notes :

Weekly Planner

Friday

To Do :

Notes :

Saturday

To Do :

Notes :

Sunday

To Do :

Notes :

Weekly Planner

Monday

To Do :

Notes :

Tuesday

To Do :

Notes :

Wednesday

To Do :

Notes :

Thursday

To Do :

Notes :

Weekly Planner

Friday

To Do:

Notes:

Saturday

To Do:

Notes:

Sunday

To Do:

Notes:

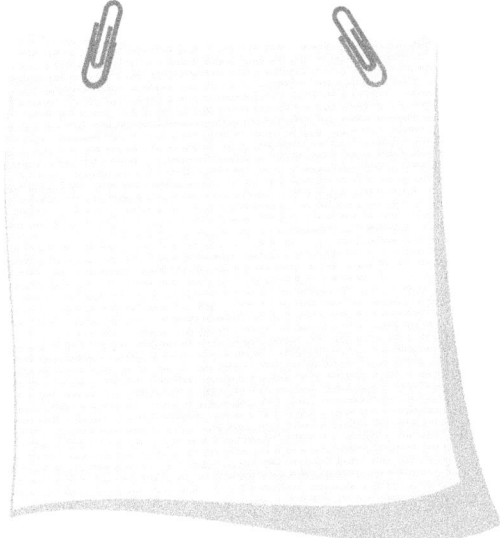

Weekly Planner

Monday

To Do :

Notes :

Tuesday

To Do :

Notes :

Wednesday

To Do :

Notes :

Thursday

To Do :

Notes :

Weekly Planner

Friday

To Do :

Notes :

Saturday

To Do :

Notes :

Sunday

To Do :

Notes :

Weekly Planner

Monday

To Do :

Notes :

Tuesday

To Do :

Notes :

Wednesday

To Do :

Notes :

Thursday

To Do :

Notes :

Weekly Planner

Friday

To Do:

Notes:
_____
_____
_____
_____
_____
_____
_____
_____
_____
_____

Saturday

To Do:

Notes:
_____
_____
_____
_____
_____
_____
_____
_____
_____
_____

Sunday

To Do:

Notes:
_____
_____
_____
_____
_____
_____
_____
_____

_____
_____
_____
_____
_____
_____

Weekly Planner

Monday

To Do :

Notes :

_____
_____
_____
_____
_____
_____
_____
_____
_____
_____

Tuesday

To Do :

Notes :

_____
_____
_____
_____
_____
_____
_____
_____
_____
_____

Wednesday

To Do :

Notes :

_____
_____
_____
_____
_____
_____
_____
_____

Thursday

To Do :

Notes :

_____
_____
_____
_____
_____
_____
_____
_____

_____
_____
_____
_____
_____
_____
_____

Weekly Planner

Friday

To Do :

Notes :

Saturday

To Do :

Notes :

Sunday

To Do :

Notes :

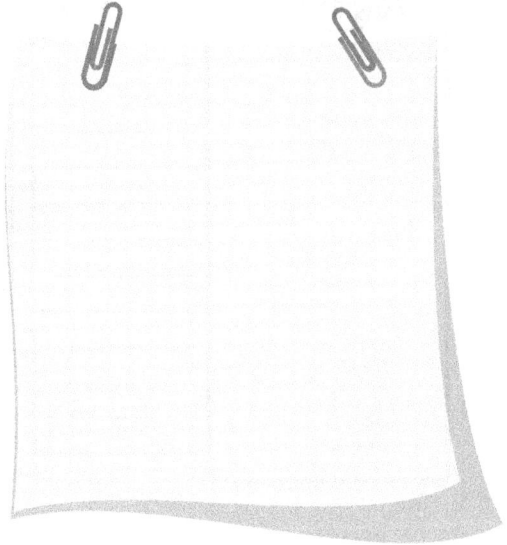

Weekly Planner

Monday

To Do:

Notes:

Tuesday

To Do:

Notes:

Wednesday

To Do:

Notes:

Thursday

To Do:

Notes:

Weekly Planner

Friday

To Do:

Notes:
_____
_____
_____
_____
_____
_____
_____
_____
_____
_____
_____

Saturday

To Do:

Notes:
_____
_____
_____
_____
_____
_____
_____
_____
_____
_____
_____

Sunday

To Do:

Notes:
_____
_____
_____
_____
_____
_____
_____
_____
_____
_____
_____

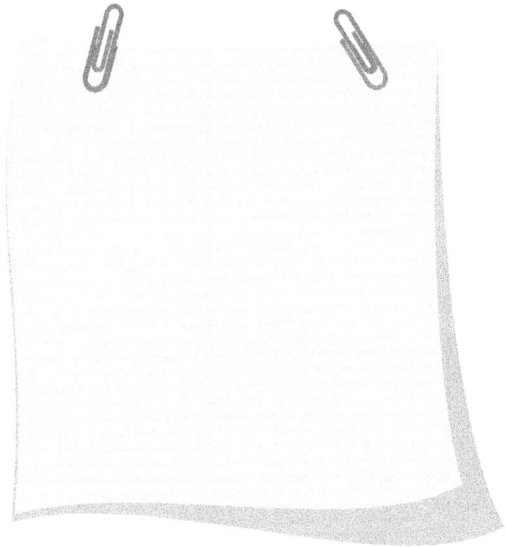

_____
_____
_____
_____
_____
_____

Weekly Planner

Monday

To Do :

Notes :
_____
_____
_____
_____
_____
_____
_____
_____
_____
_____

Tuesday

To Do :

Notes :
_____
_____
_____
_____
_____
_____
_____
_____
_____
_____

Wednesday

To Do :

Notes :
_____
_____
_____
_____
_____
_____
_____
_____
_____

Thursday

To Do :

Notes :
_____
_____
_____
_____
_____
_____
_____
_____
_____

_____
_____
_____
_____
_____
_____
_____

Weekly Planner

Friday

To Do :

Notes :

Saturday

To Do :

Notes :

Sunday

To Do :

Notes :

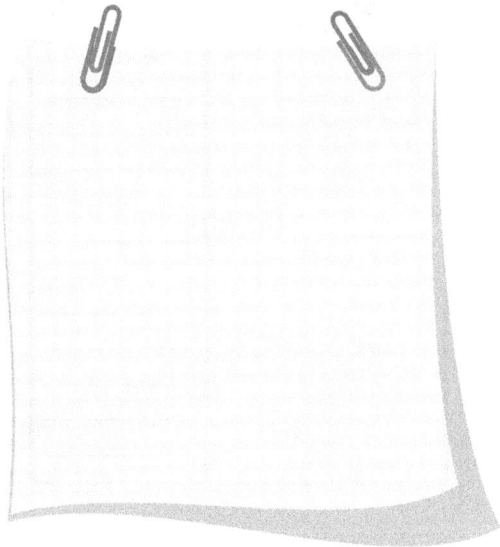

Weekly Planner

Monday

To Do :

Notes :

Tuesday

To Do :

Notes :

Wednesday

To Do :

Notes :

Thursday

To Do :

Notes :

Weekly Planner

Friday

To Do:

Notes:

_____
_____
_____
_____
_____
_____
_____
_____
_____
_____

Saturday

To Do:

Notes:

_____
_____
_____
_____
_____
_____
_____
_____
_____
_____

Sunday

To Do:

Notes:

_____
_____
_____
_____
_____
_____
_____
_____

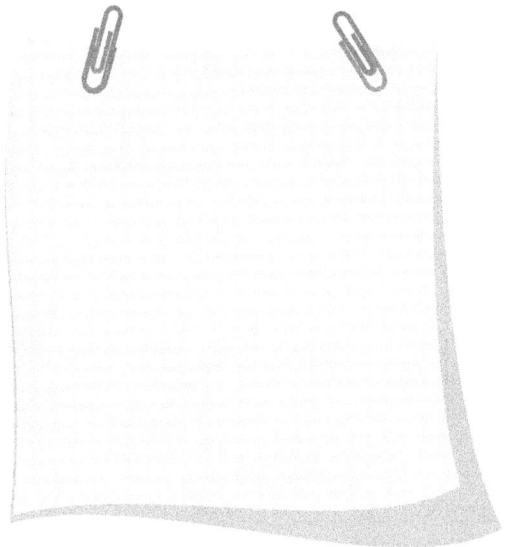

_____
_____
_____
_____
_____
_____

Weekly Planner

Monday

To Do :

Notes :

Tuesday

To Do :

Notes :

Wednesday

To Do :

Notes :

Thursday

To Do :

Notes :

Weekly Planner

Friday

To Do :

Notes :

_____
_____
_____
_____
_____
_____
_____
_____
_____

Saturday

To Do :

Notes :

_____
_____
_____
_____
_____
_____
_____
_____
_____

Sunday

To Do :

Notes :

_____
_____
_____
_____
_____
_____
_____
_____
_____

_____
_____
_____
_____
_____
_____

Weekly Planner

Monday

To Do :

Notes :

Tuesday

To Do :

Notes :

Wednesday

To Do :

Notes :

Thursday

To Do :

Notes :

Weekly Planner

Friday

To Do:

Notes:

_____
_____
_____
_____
_____
_____
_____
_____
_____
_____

Saturday

To Do:

Notes:

_____
_____
_____
_____
_____
_____
_____
_____
_____
_____

Sunday

To Do:

Notes:

_____
_____
_____
_____
_____
_____
_____
_____

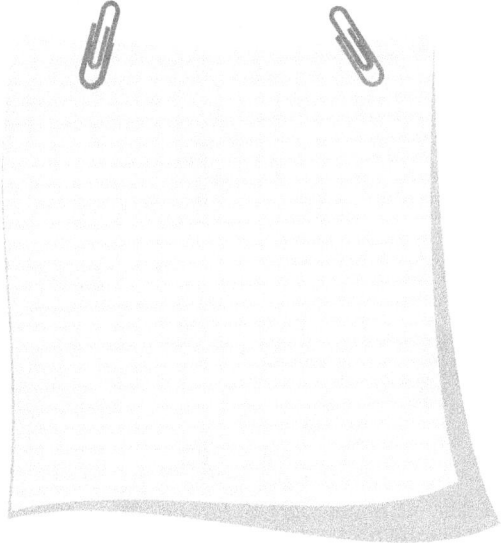

_____
_____
_____
_____
_____
_____

Weekly Planner

Monday

To Do :

Notes :

Tuesday

To Do :

Notes :

Wednesday

To Do :

Notes :

Thursday

To Do :

Notes :

Weekly Planner

Friday

To Do :

Notes :

_____
_____
_____
_____
_____
_____
_____
_____
_____
_____

Saturday

To Do :

Notes :

_____
_____
_____
_____
_____
_____
_____
_____
_____
_____

Sunday

To Do :

Notes :

_____
_____
_____
_____
_____
_____
_____
_____

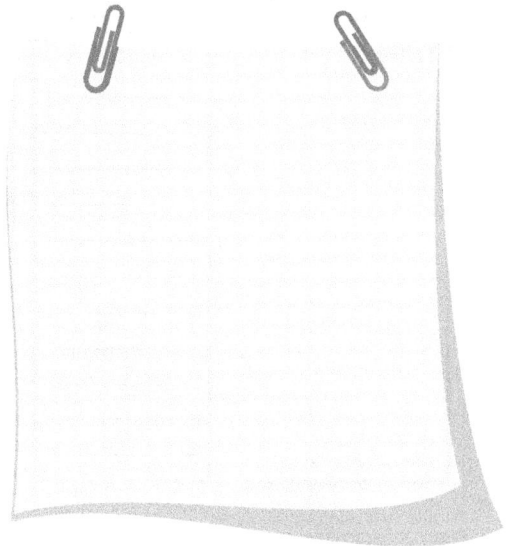

_____
_____
_____
_____
_____
_____

Weekly Planner

Monday

To Do :

Notes :

Tuesday

To Do :

Notes :

Wednesday

To Do :

Notes :

Thursday

To Do :

Notes :

Weekly Planner

Friday

To Do:

Notes:

_____
_____
_____
_____
_____
_____
_____
_____
_____
_____

Saturday

To Do:

Notes:

_____
_____
_____
_____
_____
_____
_____
_____
_____
_____

Sunday

To Do:

Notes:

_____
_____
_____
_____
_____
_____
_____
_____

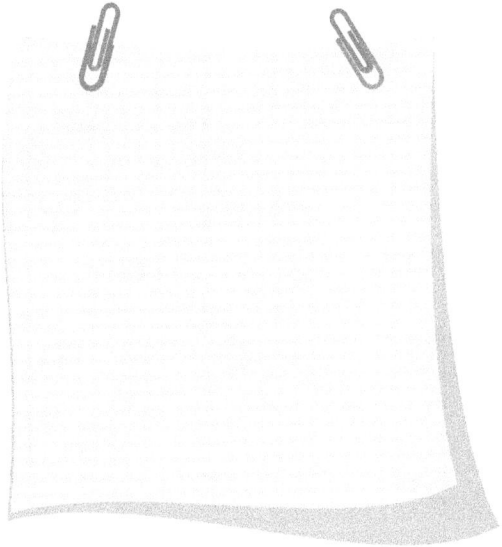

_____
_____
_____
_____
_____
_____

Weekly Planner

Monday

To Do :

Notes :

Tuesday

To Do :

Notes :

Wednesday

To Do :

Notes :

Thursday

To Do :

Notes :

Weekly Planner

Friday

To Do :

Notes :

_____
_____
_____
_____
_____
_____
_____
_____
_____
_____

Saturday

To Do :

Notes :

_____
_____
_____
_____
_____
_____
_____
_____
_____
_____

Sunday

To Do :

Notes :

_____
_____
_____
_____
_____
_____
_____
_____
_____

_____
_____
_____
_____
_____
_____

Weekly Planner

Monday

To Do :

Notes :

Tuesday

To Do :

Notes :

Wednesday

To Do :

Notes :

Thursday

To Do :

Notes :

Weekly Planner

Friday

To Do :

Notes :

_____
_____
_____
_____
_____
_____
_____
_____
_____
_____

Saturday

To Do :

Notes :

_____
_____
_____
_____
_____
_____
_____
_____
_____
_____

Sunday

To Do :

Notes :

_____
_____
_____
_____
_____
_____
_____
_____
_____
_____

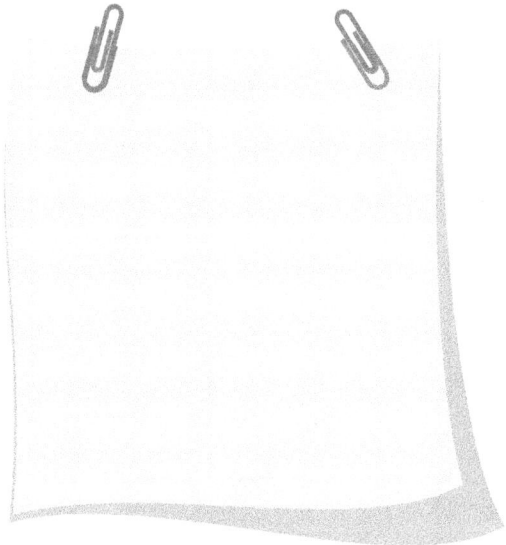

_____
_____
_____
_____
_____
_____

Weekly Planner

Monday

To Do :

Notes :

Tuesday

To Do :

Notes :

Wednesday

To Do :

Notes :

Thursday

To Do :

Notes :

Weekly Planner

Friday

To Do:

Notes:
_____
_____
_____
_____
_____
_____
_____
_____
_____
_____

Saturday

To Do:

Notes:
_____
_____
_____
_____
_____
_____
_____
_____
_____
_____

Sunday

To Do:

Notes:
_____
_____
_____
_____
_____
_____
_____
_____

_____
_____
_____
_____
_____
_____

Weekly Planner

Monday

To Do :

Notes :

Tuesday

To Do :

Notes :

Wednesday

To Do :

Notes :

Thursday

To Do :

Notes :

Weekly Planner

Friday

To Do:

Notes:

_____
_____
_____
_____
_____
_____
_____
_____
_____
_____

Saturday

To Do:

Notes:

_____
_____
_____
_____
_____
_____
_____
_____
_____
_____

Sunday

To Do:

Notes:

_____
_____
_____
_____
_____
_____
_____
_____

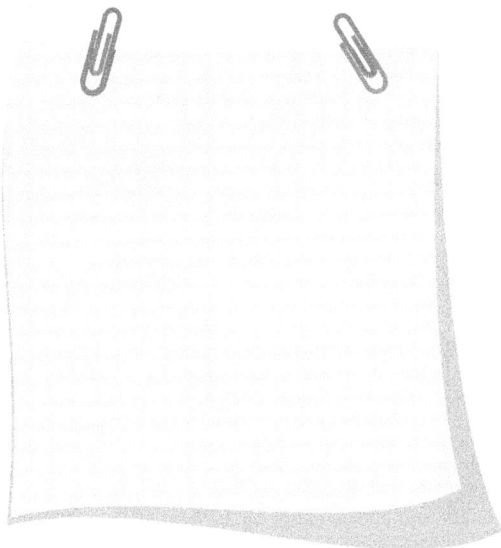

_____
_____
_____
_____
_____
_____

Weekly Planner

Monday

To Do :

Notes :

_____
_____
_____
_____
_____
_____
_____
_____
_____
_____

Tuesday

To Do :

Notes :

_____
_____
_____
_____
_____
_____
_____
_____
_____
_____

Wednesday

To Do :

Notes :

_____
_____
_____
_____
_____
_____
_____
_____
_____
_____

Thursday

To Do :

Notes :

_____
_____
_____
_____
_____
_____
_____
_____
_____
_____

_____
_____
_____
_____
_____
_____
_____

Weekly Planner

Friday

To Do:

Notes:

Saturday

To Do:

Notes:

Sunday

To Do:

Notes:

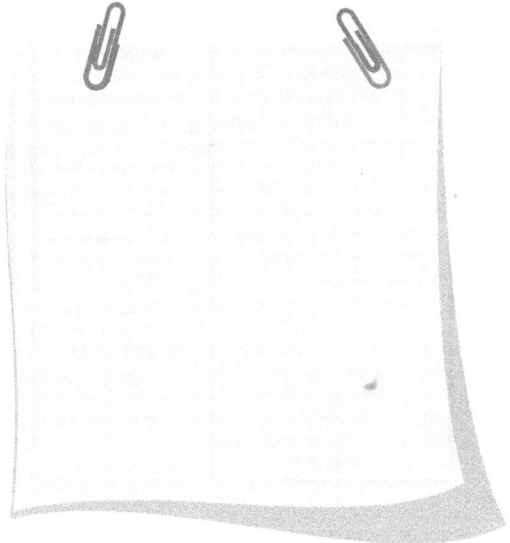

Weekly Planner

Monday

To Do :

Notes :

Tuesday

To Do :

Notes :

Wednesday

To Do :

Notes :

Thursday

To Do :

Notes :

Weekly Planner

Friday

To Do:

Notes:
_____
_____
_____
_____
_____
_____
_____
_____
_____
_____

Saturday

To Do:

Notes:
_____
_____
_____
_____
_____
_____
_____
_____
_____
_____

Sunday

To Do:

Notes:
_____
_____
_____
_____
_____
_____
_____
_____
_____

_____
_____
_____
_____
_____
_____

Weekly Planner

Monday

To Do :

Notes :

Tuesday

To Do :

Notes :

Wednesday

To Do :

Notes :

Thursday

To Do :

Notes :

Weekly Planner

Friday

To Do :	Notes :
	_____
	_____
	_____
	_____
	_____
	_____
	_____
	_____
	_____
	_____

Saturday

To Do :	Notes :
	_____
	_____
	_____
	_____
	_____
	_____
	_____
	_____
	_____
	_____

Sunday

To Do :	Notes :
	_____
	_____
	_____
	_____
	_____
	_____
	_____
	_____

_____

_____

_____

_____

_____

_____

Weekly Planner

Monday

To Do :

Notes :

_____
_____
_____
_____
_____
_____
_____
_____
_____
_____

Tuesday

To Do :

Notes :

_____
_____
_____
_____
_____
_____
_____
_____
_____
_____

Wednesday

To Do :

Notes :

_____
_____
_____
_____
_____
_____
_____
_____
_____

Thursday

To Do :

Notes :

_____
_____
_____
_____
_____
_____
_____
_____
_____

_____
_____
_____
_____
_____
_____
_____

Weekly Planner

Friday

To Do:

Notes:
_____
_____
_____
_____
_____
_____
_____
_____
_____
_____
_____

Saturday

To Do:

Notes:
_____
_____
_____
_____
_____
_____
_____
_____
_____
_____
_____

Sunday

To Do:

Notes:
_____
_____
_____
_____
_____
_____
_____
_____
_____

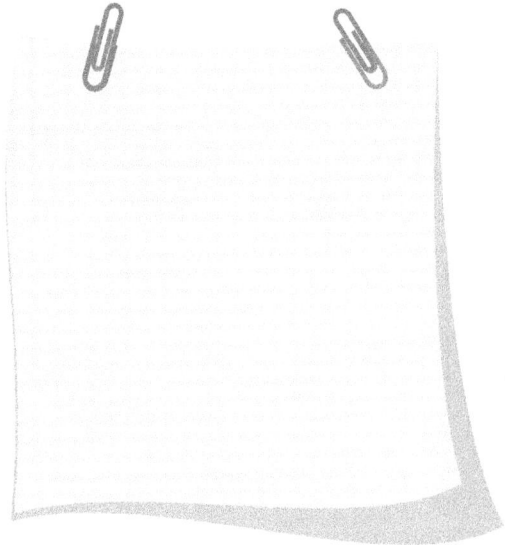

_____
_____
_____
_____
_____
_____

Weekly Planner

Monday

To Do :

Notes :

Tuesday

To Do :

Notes :

Wednesday

To Do :

Notes :

Thursday

To Do :

Notes :

Weekly Planner

Friday

To Do :

Notes :

Saturday

To Do :

Notes :

Sunday

To Do :

Notes :

Weekly Planner

Monday

To Do :

Notes :

Tuesday

To Do :

Notes :

Wednesday

To Do :

Notes :

Thursday

To Do :

Notes :

Weekly Planner

Friday

To Do:

Notes:
_____
_____
_____
_____
_____
_____
_____
_____
_____
_____

Saturday

To Do:

Notes:
_____
_____
_____
_____
_____
_____
_____
_____
_____
_____

Sunday

To Do:

Notes:
_____
_____
_____
_____
_____
_____
_____
_____

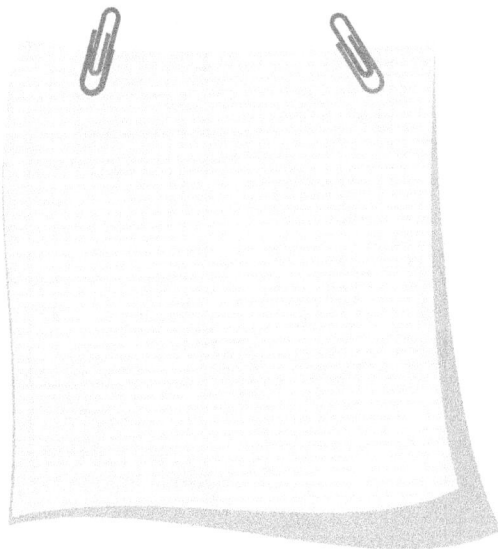

_____
_____
_____
_____
_____
_____

Weekly Planner

Monday

To Do :

Notes :

Tuesday

To Do :

Notes :

Wednesday

To Do :

Notes :

Thursday

To Do :

Notes :

Weekly Planner

Friday

To Do :

Notes :

Saturday

To Do :

Notes :

Sunday

To Do :

Notes :

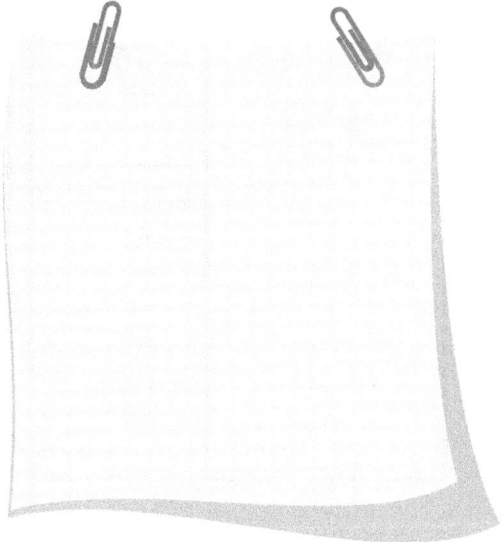

Weekly Planner

Monday

To Do :

Notes :
_____
_____
_____
_____
_____
_____
_____
_____
_____

Tuesday

To Do :

Notes :
_____
_____
_____
_____
_____
_____
_____
_____
_____

Wednesday

To Do :

Notes :
_____
_____
_____
_____
_____
_____
_____
_____

Thursday

To Do :

Notes :
_____
_____
_____
_____
_____
_____
_____
_____

_____
_____
_____
_____
_____
_____
_____

Weekly Planner

Friday

To Do :

Notes :

Saturday

To Do :

Notes :

Sunday

To Do :

Notes :

Weekly Planner

Monday

To Do :

Notes :

Tuesday

To Do :

Notes :

Wednesday

To Do :

Notes :

Thursday

To Do :

Notes :

Weekly Planner

Friday

To Do :

Notes :

Saturday

To Do :

Notes :

Sunday

To Do :

Notes :

Weekly Planner

Monday

To Do :

Notes :

Tuesday

To Do :

Notes :

Wednesday

To Do :

Notes :

Thursday

To Do :

Notes :

Weekly Planner

Friday

To Do:

Notes:

_____
_____
_____
_____
_____
_____
_____
_____
_____
_____

Saturday

To Do:

Notes:

_____
_____
_____
_____
_____
_____
_____
_____
_____
_____

Sunday

To Do:

Notes:

_____
_____
_____
_____
_____
_____
_____
_____

_____
_____
_____
_____
_____
_____

Weekly Planner

Monday

To Do :

Notes :

Tuesday

To Do :

Notes :

Wednesday

To Do :

Notes :

Thursday

To Do :

Notes :

Weekly Planner

Friday

To Do :

Notes :

Saturday

To Do :

Notes :

Sunday

To Do :

Notes :

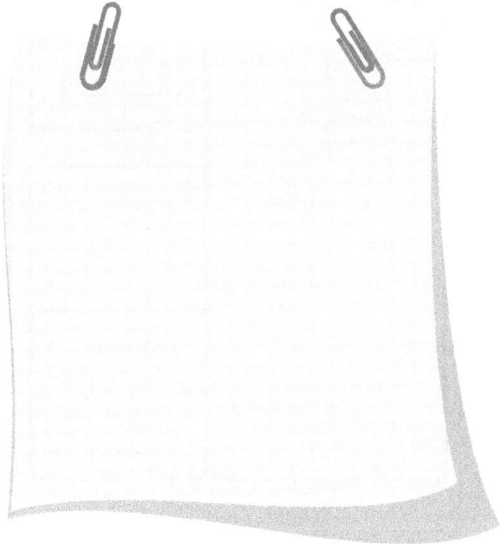

Weekly Planner

Monday

To Do :

Notes :
_____
_____
_____
_____
_____
_____
_____
_____
_____
_____

Tuesday

To Do :

Notes :
_____
_____
_____
_____
_____
_____
_____
_____
_____
_____

Wednesday

To Do :

Notes :
_____
_____
_____
_____
_____
_____
_____
_____
_____
_____

Thursday

To Do :

Notes :
_____
_____
_____
_____
_____
_____
_____
_____
_____
_____

_____
_____
_____
_____
_____
_____
_____

Weekly Planner

Friday

To Do:

Notes:

_____
_____
_____
_____
_____
_____
_____
_____
_____
_____

Saturday

To Do:

Notes:

_____
_____
_____
_____
_____
_____
_____
_____
_____
_____

Sunday

To Do:

Notes:

_____
_____
_____
_____
_____
_____
_____
_____
_____

_____
_____
_____
_____
_____
_____

Weekly Planner

Monday

To Do :

Notes :

_____
_____
_____
_____
_____
_____
_____
_____
_____
_____

Tuesday

To Do :

Notes :

_____
_____
_____
_____
_____
_____
_____
_____
_____
_____

Wednesday

To Do :

Notes :

_____
_____
_____
_____
_____
_____
_____
_____

Thursday

To Do :

Notes :

_____
_____
_____
_____
_____
_____
_____
_____

_____
_____
_____
_____
_____
_____
_____

Weekly Planner

Friday

To Do :

Notes :

_____
_____
_____
_____
_____
_____
_____
_____
_____
_____

Saturday

To Do :

Notes :

_____
_____
_____
_____
_____
_____
_____
_____
_____
_____

Sunday

To Do :

Notes :

_____
_____
_____
_____
_____
_____
_____
_____
_____

_____
_____
_____
_____
_____
_____

Weekly Planner

Monday

To Do :

Notes :

Tuesday

To Do :

Notes :

Wednesday

To Do :

Notes :

Thursday

To Do :

Notes :

Weekly Planner

Friday

To Do :

Notes :

_____
_____
_____
_____
_____
_____
_____
_____
_____
_____

Saturday

To Do :

Notes :

_____
_____
_____
_____
_____
_____
_____
_____
_____
_____

Sunday

To Do :

Notes :

_____
_____
_____
_____
_____
_____
_____
_____

_____
_____
_____
_____
_____
_____

Weekly Planner

Monday

To Do :

Notes :

Tuesday

To Do :

Notes :

Wednesday

To Do :

Notes :

Thursday

To Do :

Notes :

Weekly Planner

Friday

To Do :	Notes :
	_____
	_____
	_____
	_____
	_____
	_____
	_____
	_____
	_____
	_____

Saturday

To Do :	Notes :
	_____
	_____
	_____
	_____
	_____
	_____
	_____
	_____
	_____
	_____

Sunday

To Do :	Notes :
	_____
	_____
	_____
	_____
	_____
	_____
	_____
	_____

_____
_____
_____
_____
_____
_____

Weekly Planner

Monday

To Do :

Notes :

Tuesday

To Do :

Notes :

Wednesday

To Do :

Notes :

Thursday

To Do :

Notes :

Weekly Planner

Friday

To Do :

Notes :

Saturday

To Do :

Notes :

Sunday

To Do :

Notes :

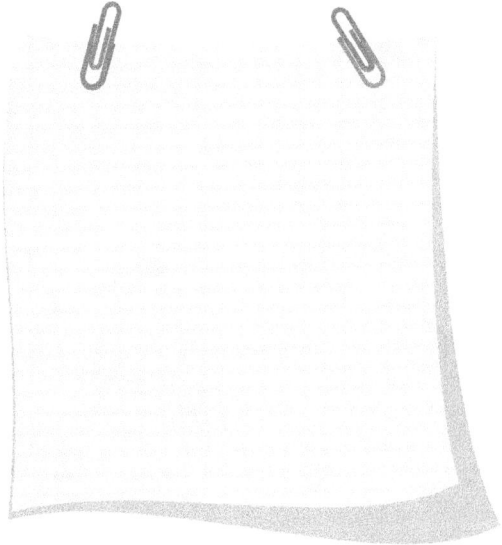

Weekly Planner

Monday
To Do :

Notes :

Tuesday
To Do :

Notes :

Wednesday
To Do :

Notes :

Thursday
To Do :

Notes :

Weekly Planner

Friday

To Do :

Notes :

_____
_____
_____
_____
_____
_____
_____
_____
_____
_____

Saturday

To Do :

Notes :

_____
_____
_____
_____
_____
_____
_____
_____
_____
_____

Sunday

To Do :

Notes :

_____
_____
_____
_____
_____
_____
_____
_____
_____
_____

_____
_____
_____
_____
_____
_____

Weekly Planner

Monday

To Do :

Notes :

Tuesday

To Do :

Notes :

Wednesday

To Do :

Notes :

Thursday

To Do :

Notes :

Weekly Planner

Friday

To Do :

Notes :

_____
_____
_____
_____
_____
_____
_____
_____
_____
_____

Saturday

To Do :

Notes :

_____
_____
_____
_____
_____
_____
_____
_____
_____
_____

Sunday

To Do :

Notes :

_____
_____
_____
_____
_____
_____
_____
_____

_____
_____
_____
_____
_____
_____

Weekly Planner

Monday

To Do :

Notes :

Tuesday

To Do :

Notes :

Wednesday

To Do :

Notes :

Thursday

To Do :

Notes :

Weekly Planner

Friday

To Do :

Notes :

_____
_____
_____
_____
_____
_____
_____
_____
_____
_____

Saturday

To Do :

Notes :

_____
_____
_____
_____
_____
_____
_____
_____
_____
_____

Sunday

To Do :

Notes :

_____
_____
_____
_____
_____
_____
_____
_____

_____
_____
_____
_____
_____
_____

Weekly Planner

Monday

To Do :

Notes :

Tuesday

To Do :

Notes :

Wednesday

To Do :

Notes :

Thursday

To Do :

Notes :

Weekly Planner

Friday

To Do:

Notes:

_____
_____
_____
_____
_____
_____
_____
_____
_____
_____

Saturday

To Do:

Notes:

_____
_____
_____
_____
_____
_____
_____
_____
_____
_____

Sunday

To Do:

Notes:

_____
_____
_____
_____
_____
_____
_____
_____

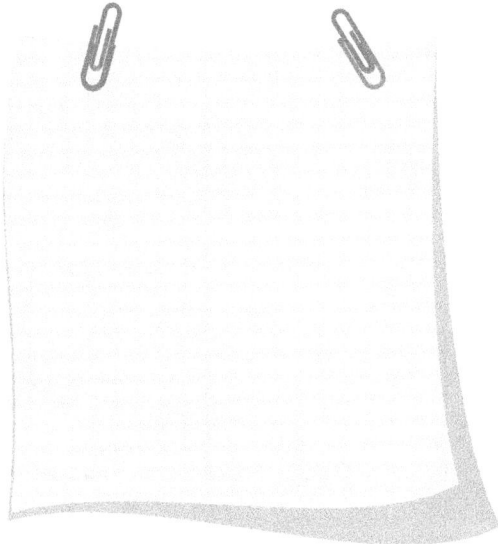

_____
_____
_____
_____
_____
_____

Weekly Planner

Monday

To Do :

Notes :

Tuesday

To Do :

Notes :

Wednesday

To Do :

Notes :

Thursday

To Do :

Notes :

Weekly Planner

Friday

To Do :

Notes :

_____
_____
_____
_____
_____
_____
_____
_____
_____
_____

Saturday

To Do :

Notes :

_____
_____
_____
_____
_____
_____
_____
_____
_____
_____

Sunday

To Do :

Notes :

_____
_____
_____
_____
_____
_____
_____
_____
_____

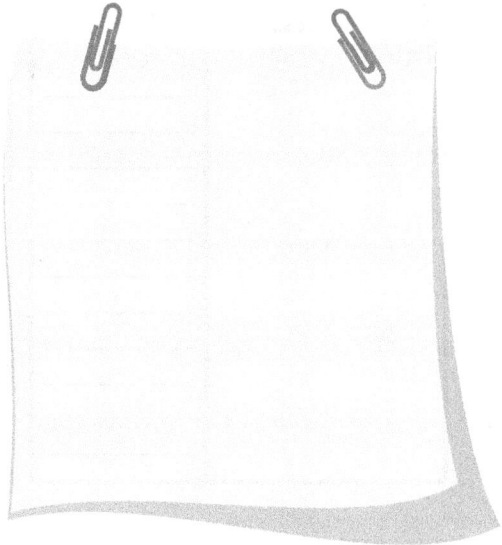

_____
_____
_____
_____
_____
_____

Weekly Planner

Monday

To Do :

Notes :

Tuesday

To Do :

Notes :

Wednesday

To Do :

Notes :

Thursday

To Do :

Notes :

Weekly Planner

Friday

To Do :

Notes :

_____
_____
_____
_____
_____
_____
_____
_____
_____
_____

Saturday

To Do :

Notes :

_____
_____
_____
_____
_____
_____
_____
_____
_____
_____

Sunday

To Do :

Notes :

_____
_____
_____
_____
_____
_____
_____
_____
_____
_____

_____
_____
_____
_____
_____
_____

Weekly Planner

Monday

To Do :

Notes :

Tuesday

To Do :

Notes :

Wednesday

To Do :

Notes :

Thursday

To Do :

Notes :

Weekly Planner

Friday

To Do:

Notes:

_____
_____
_____
_____
_____
_____
_____
_____
_____
_____
_____

Saturday

To Do:

Notes:

_____
_____
_____
_____
_____
_____
_____
_____
_____
_____
_____

Sunday

To Do:

Notes:

_____
_____
_____
_____
_____
_____
_____
_____
_____

_____
_____
_____
_____
_____
_____

Weekly Planner

Monday

To Do :

Notes :

Tuesday

To Do :

Notes :

Wednesday

To Do :

Notes :

Thursday

To Do :

Notes :

Weekly Planner

Friday

To Do:

Notes:
_____
_____
_____
_____
_____
_____
_____
_____
_____
_____

Saturday

To Do:

Notes:
_____
_____
_____
_____
_____
_____
_____
_____
_____
_____

Sunday

To Do:

Notes:
_____
_____
_____
_____
_____
_____
_____
_____

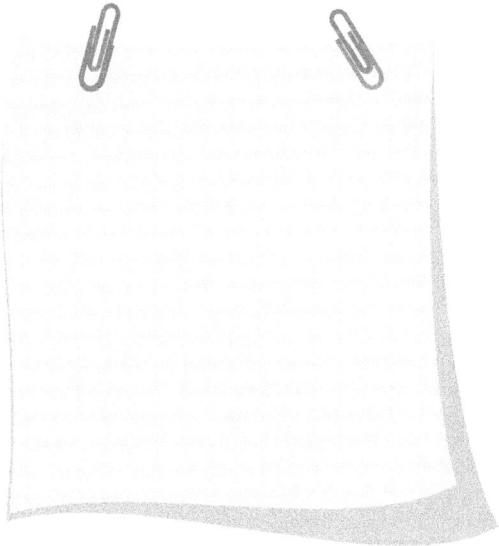

_____
_____
_____
_____
_____
_____

Weekly Planner

Notes

www.ingramcontent.com/pod-product-compliance
Lightning Source LLC
Chambersburg PA
CBHW081334090426
42737CB00017B/3132